AUREUS SOL

Burning Alive and Other Special Talents

First edition

This book was professionally typeset on Reedsy.
Find out more at reedsy.com

Contents

if I had the words, these would be it

Do you ever think about the impact you've had?
  The lives you've touched?
  Saved?

I'm not talking about pulling somebody out of the water
  I'm talking about pulling somebody out of the w a t e r

I'm not talking about performing CPR on a drowning person
  Except I am

Do you remember the time you asked me if I ate?
  Those days I had to earn my right to eat and you were there to give it to me

Do you remember the times you sat with me?
  On days I had no words to say, on days I had no one in my corner

Do you remember the times you reached towards me?
  A text, a call, a smile through the room?
  There were days I felt so invisible I thought no one could see me but you did

Do you remember the times you called someone?
You were so worried about me
There were days I thought no one would miss me but you did

Do you remember the time you gave to me?
The compassion that you shared?

Do you know the hope you gave to me when you showed me someone cared?

Do you ever think about the impact you have on someone?
Do you think think about the power of your words? Your time? Your eyes?

I am saying "how are you" can change a life, I am saying your smile saved mine

Do you know what you have done?
Do you really understand the full extent of it?

I'm talking about nights I was going to die but your voice echoes through my head whispering "one more try"

I'm talking about being nearly consumed by the darkness and you shining a light for me to follow through

Do you remember the times you talked me up?
Told me not to give up, like you really saw something in me, like I was really somebody who was gonna be somebody
You gave me importance
You really motivated me

You helped me to find confidence
You paved a path for me to meet me

Do you ever think about the lives you've saved?
Sometimes 100 in a single day

Can you recognize the force you are?

you call yourself a therapist

I invite you in
This is vulnerability grown only from desperation
I take off my skin and beg into your eyes to make something out my bones that is not so broken
You steal my identity
You crush my hope
And leave me alone
With desperate fingertips I cling to my own soul

before

Every day it's the same fucking
 Thing

Wake up to an empty fucking bed
 With an empty fucking soul

My bones are so hollow

Every day it's the same fucking
 Thing

Same fucking battle with my head

Like should I just fucking kill myself
 Or should I let myself live

say uncle

Can we lay down our defenses make amends just for tonight
I can't bear to fight another round
Raised up my claws too many times

I am over the days of wishing every symptom is the deadliest disease
I am over the days of wishing every bus will flatten me underneath it's tires
I am over the days of waiting for everyone I love to leave me

less than dirt

I woke up stuck in the trenches
I could not move no matter how bad I wanted to
Could not advance to where I want to be or anywhere at all
I kick my feet so hard to swim
I only sink quicker
I fight to make it into a lovers arms
I'm always so alone
And I can't handle the pain of rejection again so I stay hidden
Hidden behind whispers and jabs like, you'll never make it, time to face it
If you looked into my eyes you'd see the troubles that pull me deeper
Feels like sharp teeth piercing me
Where I go, I never see
I'm always covered in their spit
And when they see me I am only two inches tall
They want to use me for their show
They want me to fight
A small blind guy get taken down ya that'd be the shit right
I do not even have a space of skin left for you to dig in your nails
My holes covered in your metal tools

If I could only escape from your hands
Wash myself clean, I'd be a free man

too long

Late at night, you know I need to see you
   In my bed
   Been eternity since I've seen you

To wake again
   You know I need a reason

searching for my own hands

It's the FEELING
  I am so desperate

talking to talk

Comfort for the uncomfortable
  Strings of words strung together to fill any cracks of silence

There was a lot more to do than talk
  If you sat quiet for a moment you could feel it

losing everything

I can’t hold my shit together
   I can’t shake this hate
   So much urgency yet all I do is hurry up and wait

I can do tricks too

Pull me around on a string for a week
  Just like a puppet baby I'll stay still until you move me
  Lose the leash when I get too heavy
  Leave me to wander like a lost puppy

what are you looking for

You can find nothing if you're looking
Or you could swim to a better shore

nightmares before I sleep

At night
  The way it eats you

gonna die anyways

Too many times I've tried
  Praying for the sun
  It only rains inside

What could become of me
  When I'm crushed beneath this weight
  I keep sinking further in this pain
  I can't find an escape

On every street I seek
  Looking for a set of arms to embrace me
  For human touch I plead
  It's something that I need
  Like can you sew my seams
  I've been falling apart, leaking dark where I leave

What's the point of riches anyway
  Searching for the fame just to bury in gold chains

tell me you need me

Wait until I get you alone
  I'll tear you the fuck apart
  Bone by bone
  I'll eat every little bit
  I want you crying for me baby
  I want you begging for my spit

I know I'm out to get me

Once upon a lovesick mind
  Once upon a shipwrecked mind
  You lead me right to the water but I do not drink it
  The water is stale
  Or at least that's what I tell myself
  I don't dare
  To trust anyone more than I trust myself
  I can't dare to trust myself

a bedtime prayer

Oh I pray for a life that I don't have to pray for an escape
On so many nights and long days
Oh I pray for a life that I don't have to beg to God to take
Oh take me from this pain
Oh I beg I beg for brighter days

suicide on accident

When we used to leave a map
A trail of tears in red ink
When the blade felt like an embrace from an old friend
When we would try everything
Swimming across oceans just to drown at the shore
When there was nothing to cling to but your own hand
But the hand that's meant to feed you only bites
And you claw at your own skin desperate for a way out but only sinking further in

the hunted becomes the hunter

Fuck you, you crazy motherfucker
  I'm taking everything and I'll leave

Fuck you, you crazy motherfucker
  Don't think to look for me

Don't think my name
  Don't look my way
  Don't come looking for me

Cause you are a crazy mother fucker
  And I just have to let you be

So fuck you, you crazy motherfucker
  You really fucked things up for me

Fuck you, you crazy mother fucker
  I'm taking everything and I'll leave

And fuck you, you crazy mother fucker
  Don't think to look for me

Don't let my name cross your mind
Don't come looking, I think you'd be scared of what you'd find

just a kid

I was not a bad kid
I was just a kid

You let me down, let me drown
I was just a kid

Hiding from the truth, in your lies,
Couldn't handle it

Hiding from the truth, like the light,
An unlit candlestick

r.i.p.

To grieve
  To mourn
  A childhood lost
  Never lived

They knew
  They knew it all all along
  They ignored me
  Because I wasn't acting right
  Because I started to speak up
  Because I started to fight
  They wanted me silence
  Trampling my identity
  Feed me pills
  Defeat my will
  Until I
  Fall in line
  Just read my lines
  Until I
  Am just a puppet for you

silent prisoner

Another day more time to waste
  When every breath feels like a mistake

Pray my mom won't close the gate
  Turn her back, they take me in in chains

Don't know how I make it through the day

When the morning comes sleep past your awake
  Keep your eyes closed
  Stiff as a board now
  Don't you cry out

I can hear them in the basement
  I can hear them in the basement
  I tell the kids don't swear too much

Gold teeth with a belly underneath
  We don't say much anyways

Red eyes
  I see right behind your disguise

It's hard to face it everyday

It's harder to face this everyday

your gravestone will bring me peace

You fuck with me cause you think I'm small

Twist the dagger in your gut like a screw
  Cut the ties and turn me loose
  You're only bleeding from your own hands
  But you can blame me cause you need to
  Say it was my fault too

Cold hands to keep my heart beat
  But it doesn't beat
  I just freeze

Leave me where you want me baby
  I won't move a muscle from you

I know the house has felt so haunted
  You know we can't bring an exorcist to fight my demons
  I'm still healing
  Sometimes just breathing
  Baby I need treatment
  Call my therapist and say I'm bleeding

Murder murder murder
Why is it all so bloody around here
Make friends with the muderess just so you can get some reasons
Maybe we need a new season
With the red dripping on the white it looks evil

Bring me another quarter
Games over
When I went to hit the switch
Got a new life
Swinging through that level country 4

I can hear the ice in your glass
I can see your eyes crinkle when you laugh
So sad it's so sad
Take another shot just to make the time pass
Take another swig from the bottle baby
Take another hit for my lungs
I can smell your breath on my tongue
You know I liked you a lot better when you were passed out on the floor
Swear I'd like you a whole lot better if you were sleeping in the morgue

sunless

When I didn't know ,what's the difference
  I said it doesn't matter but I'm listening

I was angry I could feel it in my jaw, my teeth
  My bones
  Grown accustomed to a life I don't want part of
  I plead to god please cut me slack now
  Can you please send a rope I been sinking all alone
  When you keep trying to climb
  Reach a better life
  Don't need all the stars just need their light

How can we make it through without the sun
  Without anyone
  At all

With no relief with no reprieve
  What will I do who will I turn to
  If anyone

nothing

When there wasn't a reason to get out of bed anymore in the morning
Nothing awaiting
No one
No love
No sun
Only work to be done
And what was I now but just a puppet for their operations

I used to have a mind that harbored dreams I used to dream of dreams
But they hated it
They said I'd never make them
Just stay still and settle for what you have

my skin is a jail cell

I am so unsafe
  So uncomfortable in my own skin
  Like always itching, always itching on every inch even within
  I am so uncomfortable like scratching
  Clawing
  To get out of my own skin
  It's suffocating
  My own skin suffocates me
  I DROWN in it
  Like an overpowering wave
  I'm trapped beneath

How lovely you make me feel
  When you touch me when you look at me
  How so much better you make me feel when I am alone I can't even touch my own skin

crimes of sadness

Like we don't even have minds
  Ignoring all the signs
  All you wanted was our silence

Falling into lines
  Following behind
  All you wanted was compliance

Feeding us your lines
  Doctors orders fall behind
  Swallow lies or it's violence

White coats leading blind
  Closing all your eyes to the crimes
  This is violence

All you wanted was the lines
  Walking us in lines
  With our heads down
  Silent

let me out

Fed up with all the lies they feed you in the institution
Oh all you dream about now is a revolution

aimless

Pull the knife out my back just so I can move forward
Without you here I've nothing to look toward

victim of my own cannibalism

I am chewing the skin off of my lips
The nails off of my fingertips
Teeth peel me apart
Gnaw me to remains
Just the outline of me
Just a remnant of me
Until I am just blood dripping from the bone

I'm gnawing leaf from limb to root
I choke
White teeth painted red
They gnash
Blood on bone
Peel away the skin

pieces of a human

I'm dissembled
  Just pieces of myself, breaking off into bits
  I'm not even solid
  I'm melting or dissipating into air
  I am lost inside myself

doctor doctor

My baby my angel
You cut me wide to drain my blood
I'm just your game board for my own operation
But you're not even a doctor baby why don't you leave that knife alone when you're just playing
Remove each organ so carefully intentionally
You unstitch me entirely
Call it love or just bad intentions

Disassemble me bone by bone
My lover
My love you steal my coat my clothes
Leave me naked and exposed
Tearing the skin right off my bones
I was once a bag of bones
Now what's remained I'm just loose bones
Just a pile of loose bones

Leaving me alone with a sour aftertaste of regret

don’t wake me with the morning light

Now they watch me through the night
  I tell them that I’ll be alright
  They know I’m lying, I am lying

I pray to god to take my life
  I do this every fucking night
  I’m trying oh yeah I’m trying

burning leaves

Green grass for your bare feet
Purple flowers, yellow and white ones too
Sunshine to warm your naked skin
A lover's hand to hold
A day when it was 80 in October
The leaves burn red overhead
A day when there was less to forget and more to remember
A day when you didn't spend the whole day wishing you were as dead as the leaves burning red overhead

we did our best

Is it okay to say we tried
  We can't lay here suffocating in our blame
  Another broken promise another night I lay in shame

you were heaven

And when you've already been to heaven
Experienced greatness greater than greatness
Bursting through the seams with love, love!
When you've held the most beautiful work of art in your own two hands
Brushed back that hair with your own fingers attached to your hand
When you've heard your name sung through the lips of an angel
When there's been love
Real real extraordinary amounts of love
Love that felt safe and light and hopeful
Love that was being wrapped up into a bear hug, picked up into those arms, and tossed around and spun up in the air until we're both laughing too hard to continue
Love that feels like adoration, and getting close within our heads
Love that felt like I fucking got you, like we can work whatever out, because I love you, how can anything matter but love? But us?

let it out

Sometimes I break walls
  I have sorrow
  It finds its way out
  Well it's better than drowning in it in my head
  Well it's better than choking to death on my spit

I taste blood from my hand guess we're starving again
  In through windows blow hope but it's colder than dreams

days that look like nights

When days were brighter
And I were too
Days I didn't stay up all night missing you

I'm not the only masochist

Well now go ahead like you didn't need something
Like you didn't need something just to throw it all away

Well now go ahead like you didn't leave something
Like you didn't leave something cause you were scared it wouldn't stay

Well now go ahead like you didn't leave something
Like you didn't leave something just to make you bleed

spider web girl

How it's always so dark in my head
How I'm just a spider caught in my own web

circles

I never move at all
I swim in circles
I exert all of my energy just trying to keep my head above the water
I am never floating
I am sinking
Always sinking
I never move at all
Over again I just hit the wall
The wall
The wall

closer than close

Holding you close to me so I know you better
  I want our skin kissing
  I want our bones caressing

I'm aching for your touch, to hold you close to me
  I want nothing between us, only your air to breathe
  When you touch me, you breathe life into me
  I want our skin kissing, our bones caressing
  Waking up in the morning just a little more gently

I'll act desperate if you need to know I need this

Erase the hesitancy
  I need you like the air I breathe

all dogs go to heaven

27, 27...
All dogs go to heaven
But will I?
I haven't always been the good guy
But I still try
Most of the time I'm on the ground sometimes I fly
What a lie, what a line
Whisper sweet nothings into my ear while we lie
Man I wish I lived in heaven but I am too afraid to die
Sand cones and pine paper
I wish I could wake up from this dream, and save it for later
Wake up from a new day and it's still the same old scene
Wake up with your old ways and we start a new routine

In your new ways
With an old face
I gotta jet
Disassemble all my bones so I can feel intact
Bleeding out my oldest blood so that I can feel relaxed

Can I get a new line here
Wake up on a different day, it's still the same old nightmare

Pinocchio eyes

Your eyes with sticks that bore right to me
You have me over just to lose me

highway to hell

Can't you see how bad I want this
Desperation like I'm hanging from the last word of your sentence
What's your question?
I repave all the dusty roads in hopes that we find new endings
What's the greater cost here?
A broken heart, a lifetime of love
In my greatest lifetime I couldn't dream this up
A life of you and me
It's my greatest fantasy

But you're so guarded
Dare I cross it
We run the circles time and time again we're losing options

If I had one last chance
How deeply I regret
The pain of waking up without you close
The hole inside me keeps on growing

What it's like to lose everything that you've just given up
Fucking up the very best

  Failing every test just to prove a point
  I am not deserving

Can you just even out the score
  Settle down for a war
  Pull the knife out of your back and cut my heart out

I'm on the highway to hell
  What's the point in pacing myself

clown face

Paint your smile on
  Fake the get along
  So many eyes to please
  So many lies to feed
  Recite another line like "I'm just tired" "Yeah I'm fine"

Giving all your energy just to make the right impression
  Give a smile and a wave as you slowly sink under

Giving all I've got just so you don't think I'm losing what I've already lost

kayaking in the dark

How much longer can I paddle up and down the same stream
   How much longer until I run out of steam
   How much longer until I wake up
   Maybe I only live in nightmares maybe I've never had a dream

Darkness in a dream
   Sometimes I'm dead inside my dreams
   I can't escape this scene
   Leave your finger off repeat
   Back and forth
   How long I paddle up and down the same stream

for my momma

There are days I stay alive just because I know it'd hurt you too much if I didn't

hell is in the mind

Am I still alive
  Is this hell
  I can’t tell

I can't tell you how much it hurts

Baby I can not be silent much longer
  Baby I can't go without trying much longer
  I miss you so much it hurts
  Everything lacks meaning

snakes in the grass

Feeling like a snake when I'm in the grass
  See me look ahead but I keep seeing past
  Lost everything I had now I can't see past

If I move again could I ever trust a thing
  Waking up out of a dead sleep if the phone rings
  All the ways we felt alive haunt us in our dreams

If this isn't death then why am I a ghost
  If this isn't hell then what am I burning for

See me pass through days like I'm meant to
  I don't feel a thing like I'm supposed to
  If I look alive I'm successful
  We can fool them all if we have to

society eats dreams

Is it really that normal to let a man turn into mush
Let his dreams to turn into dust
We crush him until he wants nothing now

stand on my head to get to where you want to be

I helped you along
  Now I can’t find you
  Now I won’t find you
  Now I will cry

lonely soldier

Make my way through the belly of the beast
  Alone I go
  Not a familiar face in sight

remember me

How could you forget me
  Did it not mean everything
  Even if for only a little while
  Wasn't it real the way you loved me

torture: waking up without you

Dreams about you
Shards of glass to my heart
When I wake up your beautiful face is gone
I don't know the last time I heard something come out of your mouth that wasn't a lie
And I don't know the last time I touched you
My arms feel so cold without your warmth to hold onto

tell me it was just the booze

No one will help me
They're all just dirty monsters
Wish someone showed me
How to be a little stronger
What I keep hoping
That I can get along without you
...that I won't end alone without you

Baby can I come home soon
I know that bottle put you in such a sad mood
Baby let me come just kiss your wounds
Living life without a try gonna die soon

ready to flee

I left one foot on the ground
  You told me you'd be around
  You didn't stay

you had your chance

But when I'm gone don't say you wish there was something you could've done
I cried to you
You turned your head

reality is what you believe

**It's about acknowledging their reality without accepting it as your own

how long has it been

The beast makes eyes
  Move to me

I'm on edge exit planned
  I don't stand
  You look the same
  You seat alonc
  Past the years
  Daggers go through me

nothing lasts

I pray to god for better days
Have I had them all?
Is the rest a waste?

I need a reason
To keep breathing
To keep on forward
Something to look toward

I pray to god, please be a god
Should I just stop?
If I reach the end

I'm doomed either way
Fuck this fate
My heart keeps bleeding
Desperate for meaning

How can I keep believing
In god? In anyone? In me?

empty

My heart burns
   Holes
   I once held it all

I either have too much confidence or none at all

death by demons

Let the years pass us by
I'll go unseen I'll go unmissed
Wait forever just to die
We both know why
Victim to the disease
It strangled me I had no air to breathe
Fight the beast I struggle so hard to win
With an anchor thrown around my neck I try to swim
Can't do my best
Fail every test
I'm such a mess

Defeated by my demons
Say you love me never see me

I can't do it
I can't do it
Tie my noose and set me loose I
Pray to wake up on the other side
With an empty mind

I run too fast to never keep up

How I want to life to slow down
Sometimes stop altogether

windmills

Orange flowers
  Purple too
  Side of the road my view

Tell me why I pass a tree I picture my neck in a noose

Windmills blowing in the breeze
  Or blowing a breeze

Tell me why I think of you and I'm consumed
  Consumed
  To my doom

suicide notes I'll never write

I really wish I didn't have so much to say before I drown beneath the world around me
I wish I could go a day or more I barely pass by your door
Or the street
Where we grew up on
Together
Turned some cold bones into new sweaters
Kissed some cuts
Tried our best
At times
Get me through like the worst of the times
Then you lead me into the worst of times
I'm like
Wow
Do I really love so much to get tossed to the side of it
The side of it all
Throw back the curtain
I'm waiting to fall
Off the stage
I lead a life I make myself
Because damn sure none of these razor edged teeth ever did a damn thing but tear at me

Raise up a boot
Draw a sword or something hard enough to crush
Your fucking heart
When you come around
I didn't want to drown you in anything but my love
But you fucking stole it all
Left me fucking empty inside oh my god I'm starving
Fill me whole please
I need your soul please
911 it's my emergency
Kill me slowly
I will not Rest In Peace
If this is the edge I'm jumping
Take me far from nothing
I just wanted to be something
That you'd miss
Let you forget
This is my edge
Call me back I dare you to
Reel me in
I've died within
If you could only have my back when I needed you
Let's not pretend
You do me wrong and you won't let me go
Hold on my reins
Drive me insane
Lead my strings I'm just your puppet
Lead me on
You lead me on
Lead me on leave me behind
Leave me to die

I cannot lie
Without your love I can't see through the fog
I try
On and on
Don't get me wrong
I keep keeping on
Don't get me wrong
I'm just tired

bones at best

Trying my best to forget
  I'm not a ghost
  Maybe at best, a stack of old bones
  Beneath a long coat
  I wear your rope around my neck
  So I won't spill

Tell me I'm stupid
  I guess it's obvious I'm still hanging by your noose

it helps me sleep

My sister told you I was sick
In high school I slit my wrists
I am dressed in black
I don't sit inside the class

Bathroom I scream in pain
Bloody veins, a bloody blade

Crying in the rain
They have labeled me insane
Pop pills so I'm the same
Why is everyone the same?
If I told you bout the pain could you look at me the same?

Everyday I want to die
When I remember every night

My dad is screaming through the walls
In the dark I watch it all
It helps me sleep
It helps me sleep
When I hear him coming down the hall

I hold my breath and pray to God
Can I find peace
Can I find peace

My momma told me I'd be all
I don't even live at all
I just stay fastened to these walls
I feel like a sheep
Feel like a sheep

December hits us once again
I love you like my only friend

Time's never moved so slow
I have never felt so old
Why'd you have to make me go
Fucking never ending cold
Now I'm nothing but a ghost

It helps me sleep
It helps me sleep

wrap me in lies

Blinding lights
  Darting eyes
  Wrap me in lies

To make it through
  I need something to cling to

Look at me let my knees go weak
  Build a fantasy where my dreams can breathe
  Recite your lines to me like you've practiced them for weeks
  Leading me on without any eyes to see

When I start to need you more you leave me stranded

You have me right where you want me
  Pin down my wings with just a finger

I held your best interest, you held no answer

Can I rest now and say I tried
  I tried my best
  Most nights I lay alone I wish I'd die

I need more rest than sleep provides

When I see you, act like a lover
You leave again
My bones feel hollow
Am I stuck in love, or just stuck in the void
Only a second goes by, eternity in my mind

Loneliness eats me
In our bed your ghost won't leave me

When I see your face I want to touch it
And it breaks

I'm craving your skin and some conversation

I need you to let me in, you keep fighting for a way out

My lungs lay still without your air
When you're gone I can't fucking care

I'm a fucking fake
Please don't look at me that way

I am fucking sick
Gouge my eyes
And slit my wrists

Read between the lines
Will you find what you missed

You trust me to wait and change
  Like I'm just at your disposal babe

blood like bricks

I feel weighed down
  Even my blood feels heavy

only alive in my dreams

I know what it's like to not be seen
Invisible to the eye
I'm alive only in my dreams
Pour an empty bottle down the drain
Throw my guts up with my lungs
Smoking until I feel so numb
Blood keeps pouring but I feel so numb

I keep keeping on but what cost
You hold me on your shoulder but I'm still lost

to be let down again would kill me

I am in so much pain mentally and physically
It doesn't end
That's not the point
We feel pain as reminder to move
Make moves, make a difference, find better ways to keep on living, loving, forgiving

Where do we start
Put myself back together before we all fall apart
I can't see straight
Out of the dark it's a long road
I don't know if I'll reach the end
Isn't that the point?

I feel all alone on this ride
They're all just passerby's

Grab the lights when you see them
I need me like a million more reasons
To keep dreaming

Is it all for nothing

I don't see a way out
Claws on the walls maybe it's just my demons

None of my friends like me
They never call
My family write me say they miss me
Where do I fall
I hangout near the bottom, never a priority at all

Maybe some of them have the same shit going on
Where they can't get through a day or night without feeling they've done it all wrong

But I'm so alone
So alone
So
So
Alone

I can't trust anyone
They don't like me

Keep me at a distance
I can't be let down again
It would kill me

Leave me here
So alone
So alone
So alone

I can’t be let down again
It would kill me

we must keep going

I don't know where I should go all along I've felt alone
  Like I have no one
  Nobody to rely on who's my friend when I'm crying
  When I'm dying
  All alone

Meet me in my private lair
  Death is knocking at our door
  With a fire
  Burning brighter than before

What's in hell
  I wish I'd find
  Out from someone
  Before I'm going

So can we just lay down our guards
  Settle the score
  No one is winning anyway
  With a vengeance

Crying out from up above

This is to the ones I love
I am sorry

For all the pain I let you see
Sometimes it's leaking out of me
Sew the darkness
Back inside me
I'm better off drowning in silence

Draw the blinds
Won't share the key
If I only let you see all the good side
Would you still call me

I'm feeling sorry
Throw my weight from ship to sea
I'll be trying
To keep us floating
We must keep going

dead end

How much longer can we make it down the same road
  How I'm looking for a way out, all the exits closed

If it isn't too much to ask
  Close my eyes until the lights burnt out

A rabbit hole
  I can't escape at all
  And I look for signs of life in everything but me

professional actress

"I'm fine"
I lie,
It's just my line
I get by

Make it through
I've gotten used to this

sunsets make me cry

One hour I am laughing in the sun
  Then I'm watching it set
  From the bathroom window
  Crying and I need it all to end

I miss everyone I ever met

That's me, though, the lover
The loner, the leave-ee, not the leaver
The overly attached
I need you now and forever
I can't think straight when you're not around because I miss you so bad
All I can think about is how bad I miss you
I love everybody
I miss them all forever
If I loved you once I'll always miss you
For eternity now you are a part of me

waiting to be loved

Each moment with you I am grateful for
I do not live with expectation of their being a next
I do not ask, I do not wonder
I find peace and comfort in this one and when the next look comes, I find it again
I stay steady and comfortable in my own skin with my own heart beating in my own chest
I find my own rhythm
And I stay steady so when you're ready I'll be here again
It takes a lot to stay so still but even more to go
Let the bird out of the cage
Free from one thing, imprisoned by a hundred more
Metal bars to keep you out
I have such little doubt that I'll be able to make it beyond them or beyond much of anywhere
If it was worth the move
It keeps me up at night
How can I leave empty handed
I came home to be bandaged
To walk away barely standing?
I've been broken and broken again, left, abandoned
I feel stranded

And every piece of me I cling to is another reason I can't move, again
If I can't forgive what I have done it's not likely I'll get through it
I'm ruined
What a storm we whether forever fighting to be free
It's never ending
A battle I'm far from out running
Oh, and what a beautiful day to sing about the crows
Or new bones
Growing under my skin
I've had a good reason to sing about a wage less war
If I tried to fight you back I'd hate to settle the score
Settle down and write another letter to your best friend or your sister
Someone's always calling and you have a new voicemail
Try again
I've been up since 2 and I can't go on without seeing
Do your best just this once for me, turn on the light
I'm blinded, let's see
If something tried to love and leave you maybe you'd just fucking eat it whole instead
Leave you for dead
Fuck that
Can you risk that?
I'm worth a lot more than a gamble

pointless

You'll never see me again anyways
What's the point
I think we lost the chance of having one

ashamed of my shadow

It’s embarrassing when I can’t tell you what I do to hide the pain
And I can’t show myself when I hide even from the mirror

not again

How do you live with yourself
I wake up and wish I didn't

on repeat

Baby I felt like we were going nowhere fast
If you said it once you probably thought about it a few times
I'm not really one to beg or promise you something I'll regret later
I didn't mean anything by it
Next time when you come around, leave me out of it
I've been here for a time or two
Something's always changing
Nothing's new
Rewind the tape just to get lost in a scene again
Each time we pass your face I press pause and then replay
Baby read your line again
Each night I spend a little less time thinking of the finer things
I'm stuck when the sun hits your eyes
I think if I could just read your mind I'd find my own way out

your signature move

Pull me in just to push me away

raining again

Rain falls on my plate
  I keep wishing for a brighter day

leftovers

I'm not a priority in the slightest

An after thought
  Leftovers

Just a warm body to crawl into bed next to
  After a drunken night

And I wonder why I'm never enough
  I'm never worth the fight

And I wonder why I can't fucking leave when all you do is cause me strife

Cut the strings you've tied me to
  I am so sick of hanging at the end of your noose

Well I'm only here for a little while longer
  And I'll leave quietly

How the fuck do you have such a hold on me
  When I look at you you feel fucking nothing

My heart's always racing
What a waste to give it all away
And be left so hollow

You talk down at me
Like I am less
Less than

Maybe if I'm quieter
Less noticeable

I'm never noticed

I knew it was over you didn't light up anymore when you see me

leave before you're left

I know how it is
 You feel confident and excited
 All you see is wonderful possibilities

Then you get sucked in
 And it is
 Everything
 That you imagined
 But more
 And it's good
 Everything's good

But you know
 It could go
 At anytime
 No moment is guaranteed

And how do you live with that fear
 Once it's unveiled
 It's impossible to ignore

It's easier to fathom losing everything when you have nothing to lose

diseases of the mind

That anxiety is a cancer
  I get high and I'm still without the answer

Something's always missing
  When I die don't think you'll miss me

bandage me

If I can't fill this hole in me how much longer until I bleed out entirely

scripts

We all lie
To get by
Like how you doing, I'm fine
Just read your lines

off the ledge

Leave me in the dark
You tear my soul apart
Never worth a fight
Lead me on leave me behind

You push me to the edge
Can't give a fuck if I was dead
I'd rather be dead
I can't escape my head
My soul just filled with dread
Fuck everything you said
Lead my feet right off the ledge

anything you ask

I try, I try so hard for you
Bleed my reddest blood
I die like the deadest for you

nights awake

I know you say I'll be fine
  But how many nights can I lay awake waiting to die

In the darkest of the night
  I pray to God for something to cling to

chains

If you can't stay consistent just stay consistently gone
   I can't handle the back and forth
   The unknowing
   The uncertainty
   Pulls me down like a weight on me

Unreliability, you drag me down like you have fucking chains on me

And I can't even move an inch
   I'm paralyzed by you

blind without you

I've eyes for only you

please think of me

Think of me, think of me, please think of me
Desire me
Ache for me, long for me
Feel desperate for me like you need me to breathe

Past the point of needing someone to talk to
Just toss me to the side I'm old news
And when you walk on by you can just walk right through me

You cannot begin to care
Please
Save the pleasantries for someone easier to fool
I don't need to play pretend anymore

it's okay

So I'm sorry if you didn't have it all the way you wanted
I moved mountains
Calmed the oceans
You divert your eyes to dull the intensity boring through you

It's okay
We're all a little disillusioned sometimes
It's okay
Maybe love can be enough to get us by
It's okay
If you'd hang on to me I'd never leave
Maybe it'd be enough
If you just had someone to count on

fear can kill you or motivate you

I cannot forgive what I've done
  How I stayed still when I should've run

I cannot forgive who I've become
  Times I stayed still I should've run

Held down by the force of fear
  I never stood a chance

not a woman

I no longer wanted to be what they wanted me to
  I tried for many years and endured much suffering

I wished I wasn't a woman
  To be harassed to be laughed at to be objectified at all moments

To lie with clenched fists
  And held breath
  To pray I grow invisible
  Or disappear entirely

To avoid eyes
  Pretend I'm not shaking
  Pretend I'm not waiting ready to fight back
  To pray he's gone when he leaves

To tiptoe around very corner
  To pray to god that I'm not seen

When you're only five years old
  There is no safety behind closed doors

Why can't people just be calm and quiet
   Why can't people just be calm and quiet

love letters to my mother

I wish desperately to hold your face between my hands
To tell you I love you to your eyes
You are beautiful
You are extraordinary
Please do not make yourself small
You are a goddess
You are a warrior
You are the universe

www.ingramcontent.com/pod-product-compliance
Lightning Source LLC
LaVergne TN
LVHW050557160826
845677LV00011B/2347

* 9 7 9 8 8 4 7 8 4 8 8 0 0 *